Classifying Birds

ANDREW SOLWAY

Heinemann Library
Chicago, Illinois

Originated by Dot Gradations
Printed in China

07 06 05 04
10 9 8 7 6 5 4 3 2

Library of Congress Cataloging-in-Publication Data
Solway, Andrew.
   Classifying birds / Andrew Solway.
      p. cm. -- (Classifying living things)
Summary: Explains what birds are and how they differ from other animals, with descriptions of various types of birds, including birds of prey, water birds, and exotic birds.
Includes bibliographical references (p.   ) and index.
   ISBN 1-4034-0844-0 (lib. bdg. : hardcover) -- ISBN 1-4034-3344-5 (pbk.)
   1. Birds--Classification--Juvenile literature. 2. Birds--Juvenile literature. [1. Birds.] I. Title. II. Series.
   QL677 .S66 2003
   598--dc21

                                                           2002015401

Acknowledgements
The publishers would like to thank the following for permission to reproduce photographs:
pp. 4 (left), 23 Oxford Scientific Film/Robert Tyrell; pp. 4 (right), 17 Digital Vision; p. 5 Photodisc; p. 7 Oxford Scientific Film/David M. Dennis; p. 9 Oxford Scientific Film/Michael Dick/AA; p. 11 Nature Picture Library/John Downer; p. 12 Oxford Scientific Film/Mark Hamblin; p. 13 Oxford Scientific Film/Norbert Rosing; p. 14 Oxford Scientific Film/Daniel Cox; p. 15 Oxford Scientific Film/Mary Plage; pp. 16, 21 Nature Picture Library/John Cancalosi; p. 18 Oxford Scientific Film/Kjell Sandved; p. 19 Oxford Scientific Film/Doug Allen; p. 20 Digital Stock; p. 22 Corbis/Eric and David Hosking; p. 24 Corbis/Fritz Polking; p. 25 Oxford Scientific Film/Daybreak Imagery; p. 26 Oxford Scientific Film/Konrad Wothe; p. 27 Corbis/Francis G. Mayer; p. 29 Natural History Museum/Michael Long.

Cover photograph of white pelicans reproduced with permission of Oxford Scientific Films.

For Harriet, Eliza, and Nicholas.

The publishers would like to thank Martin Lawrence, museum educator, for his assistance in the preparation of this book.

Some words are shown in bold, **like this.** You can find out what they mean by looking in the glossary.

Contents

The Variety of Life

The world is full of an incredible variety of living things. They range from tiny bacteria too small to see, to huge redwood trees more than 325 feet (100 meters) tall. With such an amazing variety of life, it can be hard to make sense of the living world. That's why scientists classify living things. That is, they sort them into groups.

Sorting the living world

When you sort things, you need to do it in a useful way. Scientists try to classify living things in a way that shows how one group of animals or plants is related to another.

Scientists who sort birds look at all the differences among them, from the color of their feathers to the shape of their bones. They also look at **fossils** of birds that lived in the past, to see which modern birds they resemble. From all this information, they decide which birds are closely related and which are not.

From kingdoms to species

Scientists divide living things into huge groups called **kingdoms**. Plants, for example, are all in one kingdom, while all animals are in another.

Birds range in size from tiny hummingbirds to ostriches, which can grow to a huge 8 feet (2.5 meters) tall.

Each kingdom is divided into smaller groups called **phyla,** and phyla are further divided into **classes.** The next subdivision is into **orders,** then **families,** then **genera,** and finally **species.** A species is a single kind of animal or plant, such as a swallow or a buttercup.

Scientific names

Many living things have a common name. But common names are not always exact, and they can be different in different languages. The bird called a robin in Europe, for instance, is different from an American robin.

To help with any confusion, scientists give every species of living thing a two-part Latin name that is the same all over the world. The two names are sort of like your first name and last name. The first name is the name of the genus that the creature belongs to. The second is the name of the species within that genus. For example, the American robin has the name *Turdus migratorius*, while the European robin is *Erithacus rubecula*.

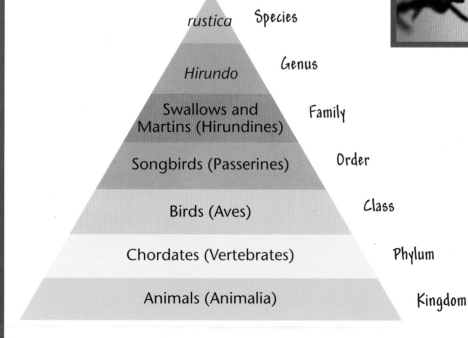

rustica	Species
Hirundo	Genus
Swallows and Martins (Hirundines)	Family
Songbirds (Passerines)	Order
Birds (Aves)	Class
Chordates (Vertebrates)	Phylum
Animals (Animalia)	Kingdom

This diagram shows the full classification for Hirundo rustica, a swallow.

What Are Birds?

We classify living things according to how closely they are related. Birds are all related to each other because they all have one group of **ancestors** that lived millions of years ago.

How birds fit in

Birds are part of the animal **kingdom.** Animals, unlike plants, cannot make their own food and must eat other living things to stay alive. Birds are part of a **phylum** called the **vertebrates.** Like us, birds have backbones. This is what makes them vertebrates.

Evolving and adapting

Scientists believe that over thousands or millions of years, groups of living things change, or evolve, to fit in better with their environment. This happens because living things that are better **adapted** to their environment live longer and produce more offspring than those that are not. All the birds we see today probably evolved from a single ancestor.

What makes a bird a bird?

Scientists have found several important differences between birds and other vertebrates. By looking at all the differences together, we can tell whether an animal is a bird or not.

Other vertebrates may have smooth skin, or they may be scaly or hairy. But birds are the only animals that have feathers. Most vertebrates have bony jaws and usually teeth as well. Birds, however, all have a horny beak.

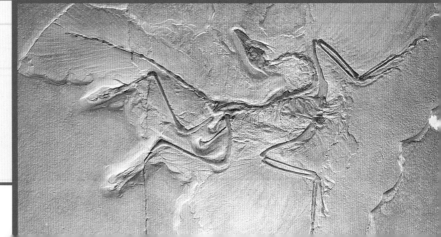

Fossils teach us about birds that lived millions of years ago. This bird, Archaeopteryx, *lived about 150 million years ago. It had wings and feathers, but its beak had teeth and its legs had claws.*

All birds have wings. Even birds that can't fly, such as ostriches, have small wings. Bats also have wings, but they are not birds—their wings are not covered with feathers.

Birds are divided into about 27 different **orders.** This table shows the main bird orders and those mentioned in this book.

Order	No. of species	Examples
Anseriformes	150	ducks, geese, swans
Apodiformes	403	swifts, hummingbirds, nightjars
Charadriiformes	257	gulls, terns, skuas, auks, snipes, sandpipers, plovers, puffins
Ciconiiformes	1,033	storks, herons, flamingos, spoonbills, ibises, albatrosses
Columbiformes	316	pigeons, doves, sandgrouse
Coraciiformes	193	kingfishers, bee-eaters, rollers, hornbills
Cuculiformes	151	cuckoos, turacos, roadrunners
Falconiformes	286	eagles, falcons, hawks, buzzards, osprey
Galliformes	256	grouse, pheasants, partridges, quails, turkeys, jungle fowl
Gruiformes	197	cranes, rails, bustards, coots
Passeriformes	5,200	sparrows, starlings, robins, finches, warblers, flycatchers, swallows, martins, wagtails, shrikes, thrushes, crows, wrens, birds of paradise, sunbirds, weaver birds
Pelecaniformes	62	pelicans, cormorants, frigate birds
Piciformes	376	woodpeckers, sapsuckers, jacamars, puffbirds, barbets, honeyguides, toucans
Procellariiformes	104	petrels, shearwaters
Psittaciformes	130	parrots, cockatoos, parakeets, lovebirds, macaws
Strigiformes	134	owls
Struthioniformes	14	ostriches, emus, cassowaries, rheas

Feathers

Birds are the only living things that have feathers. A bird would not be a bird without them. Feathers grow from a bird's skin in the same way that we grow hair or nails.

A bird's feathers do three important jobs:
- They give the bird a smooth, streamlined shape. This makes flying through the air easy, saving the bird's energy.
- Feathers on the bird's skinny arms turn them into broad, flexible wings, ideal for flying.
- Feathers on its body protect the skin from the sun in hot weather and keep it warm in cold weather.

Feather structure

Feathers have a structure that makes them very light and strong. Down the center of the feather is a hollow tube or rib. Sticking out from this rib are hundreds of thin, slanting strips called barbs. Each barb has rows of tiny teeth along its length, which link up with the teeth of the barbs on either side like the teeth in a zipper. This locks the barbs together, making the feather into a strong, flat blade.

In wing feathers, all the barbs link together in this way. But on the body, the lower part of each feather is soft and fluffy. The fluffy part of the feather helps keep the bird warm.

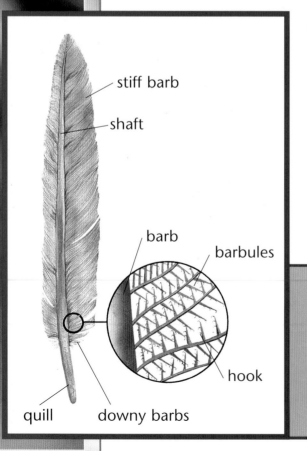

stiff barb

shaft

barb

barbules

hook

quill

downy barbs

This illustration shows the parts of a feather. The enlargement shows how the teeth on each barb lock together. Each barb has a lot of even tinier teeth, called barbules, on it. The barbules have hooks on them that zip up the barbules.

Feathers are tough, but they must be cared for and they do wear out. Birds regularly preen, or clean and comb their feathers with their beaks. Then about once a year, birds molt, which means their old feathers are replaced with new ones.

Patterns and colors

A bird's **plumage** can be almost any color, from dull browns and grays to bright reds and blues. The plumage may help the bird **camouflage** itself. Birds that live in reeds, for instance, often have a pattern of brown and black bars that makes them very hard to spot among the reeds.

Some birds have plumage that really stands out. These birds are usually male birds, and they grow brightly colored feathers to help them attract females for **breeding.** In some birds, the breeding feathers can be truly spectacular.

Birds of paradise, like this Wilson's bird of paradise, live in warm tropical forests in Australia and New Guinea. The males have spectacular feathers, which they parade in the breeding season to attract females.

Built to Fly

We have already seen that a bird's wing feathers help it to fly. But there is much more to flying than wings and feathers. From beak to tail, inside and out, birds are suited for flight.

Light bones

Compared to a land animal of the same size, a bird's skeleton is lighter and stronger. This helps it to fly. One way that a bird's skeleton is different is that it has fewer bones. Many of the bones in its back and hips are joined together. A bird's wings also have fewer bones than the arms or front feet of other **vertebrates.**

A bird's beak is another **adaptation** to save weight. Jawbones and teeth are much heavier than a bird's light, strong beak. In addition, over time birds have lost their tail bones, which has helped to balance their skeleton.

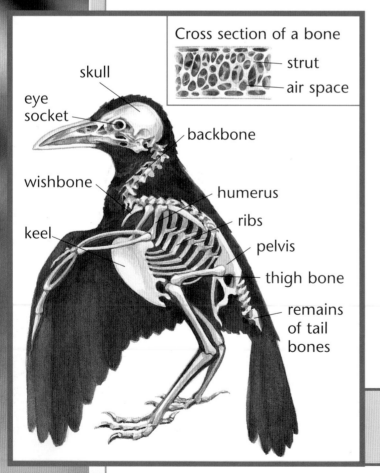

Cross section of a bone

strut

air space

skull

eye socket

backbone

wishbone

humerus

ribs

keel

pelvis

thigh bone

remains of tail bones

Many birds have bones that are lighter than those of other animals. This is because they have air spaces inside them. Bigger birds usually have more air spaces in their bones than smaller ones have. A frigate bird, for example, has a wingspan of more than 6.6 feet (2 meters), but its skeleton weighs less than its feathers! Even birds that have lost the ability to fly have fewer bones in their skeleton and a beak instead of jaws.

This is the skeleton of a bird.

Strong muscles

Although birds are light, they still need a lot of muscle power to get into the air. Nearly all a bird's muscles are concentrated in its body, because heavy muscles in the wings would make them harder to flap. The biggest muscles are the breast muscles, which flap the wings. They are attached to a broad, flat bone fastened to the ribs, called the keel.

*Every year, bar-headed geese fly over Mount Everest at heights of more than 29,500 feet (9,000 meters) on their **migration** flights. At this height, there is only a third of the amount of oxygen in the air than there is at sea level.*

A bird's legs also need strong muscles to absorb the shock of landing. All these muscles are concentrated at the tops of the legs. The legs themselves are very skinny. Flightless birds have leg muscles that are big and strong, but the muscles in the upper body are smaller, as they don't need them for flying.

Energy for flying

Birds need a strong heart and a good blood system to keep their muscles supplied with energy. Hummingbird hearts beat fastest of all—up to 1,200 times every minute! Human hearts beat about 70 times per minute. On a high mountain, humans find it hard to breathe, because there is less oxygen in the air there. But birds have no problem flying at these heights. They have very efficient lungs, which can get more oxygen from the air.

Perching Birds

More than half the bird **species** in the world are perching birds or **passerines** (**order** Passseriformes). They all have feet suited for perching, with three toes pointing forward and a strong fourth toe pointing backward. Most passerines are small or medium-sized. One or two species feed in water, but most are land birds.

Although passerines have some things in common, they come in a fantastic variety of colors, shapes, and sizes. Many common birds, for example crows, finches, sparrows, swallows, thrushes, and wrens, are passerines. But the group also includes the fabulously decorated birds of paradise, **nectar**-eating sunbirds, and impressive nest-builders such as ovenbirds and weaver birds.

Larks are quite dull-looking brown birds, but when the male lark opens its beak and starts to sing, its song is beautiful.

Songbirds

One large group of passerines are the songbirds. All birds have short calls to keep in touch or to warn of danger. In some species, male birds have songs that they sing to mark their territory or to attract a **mate.** But only songbirds have extra muscles in their voice box to help them sing. Not all songbirds are good singers. Few people would call the harsh croak of a crow beautiful, but crows are songbirds!

Passerine foods

Most passerines eat seeds, insects, or both. For instance, sparrows and finches eat mostly seeds, swallows and martins catch insects in flight, and crows and their relatives eat both kinds of food. A few passerines eat other foods, however. Sunbirds are like hummingbirds and eat nectar from flowers. Birds of paradise eat fruit. In the tropical forests where they live, fruit is available all year.

Nest-builders

Many passerines lay their eggs in cuplike or domed nests that are completely enclosed. The babies are blind and helpless when they hatch. Some passerines build really impressive nests. Male weaver birds thread together grass and plant stems to make basketlike nests. Ovenbirds build domed clay nests, which look similar to the clay ovens that people sometimes make to cook food outdoors.

A golden pale weaver builds a nest in Mombasa, Kenya. Male weavers build nests to attract females. A female will mate with the male whose nest she likes best.

Food grinder

Birds have no teeth, so they cannot chew their food. Without chewing, it is very difficult for the **digestive system** to get nutrients from food. So birds "chew" their food in their stomachs! A part of the stomach called the gizzard has very hard, muscular walls. In the gizzard, the food is churned around and ground up into small pieces. Most birds swallow small stones or grit that help to break up food.

Living on the Ground

Many birds have lost the ability to fly. Ostriches and their relatives are in the **order** Struthioniformes, which are flightless. Game birds make up another order of ground-dwellers called Galliformes. They are similar in some ways to ostriches and their relatives, but many can fly. Pheasants, quails, partridges, grouse, and Indian jungle fowl are all game birds.

Cassowaries are nearly as big as ostriches. They have a deadly kick, and the inner nail on their feet can be four inches (ten centimeters) long. More people in New Guinea are killed by cassowaries than by any other wild animal.

Ostriches

Ostriches, cassowaries, emus, and rheas are all large birds with long, powerful legs. Ostriches, emus, and rheas live in open country and are fast runners, while cassowaries are forest birds. They all feed mainly on plants and nest on the ground.

Kiwis are much smaller than their ostrich relatives and move more slowly. They hunt at night for earthworms, their favorite food. Although their eyesight is poor, they have an excellent sense of smell.

Birds as big as elephants!

Ostriches are the biggest living birds. They can grow up to 8 feet (2.5 meters) tall and weigh twice as much as an average man. Until a few hundred years ago in New Zealand there were much bigger birds called moas. The biggest grew to almost 13 feet (4 meters) tall. That's taller than an elephant!

Game birds

Birds such as pheasants, grouse, partridges, and quails have been bred and hunted for sport for many years. This is why they are called game birds. Game birds live on open ground or in forests, hunting for seeds and other plant food. They usually hide if danger threatens, but if they spot a **predator** they suddenly burst out and fly quickly upward. A grouse can fly almost vertically from the ground.

Female game birds are usually dull-colored, but some males have splendid coats of **plumage.** The peahen (a female peacock) has plain, brown plumage, but the peacock is famous for its dazzling display of colorful feathers.

Like ostriches, most game birds nest on the ground. If their young were born helpless, like those of **passerines,** they would soon be snapped up by predators. To avoid this, the young have feathers when they hatch and can move about and feed themselves right away. They can fly within a day of hatching.

In the **breeding** season, male sage grouse gather on open ground at dawn. They puff themselves up, leap, flutter, and pose to try and attract females. This behavior is called lekking.

Water Birds

On rivers and streams, ponds, lakes, and marshes, you will find birds. At the water's edge, long-legged birds fish or probe for food. Farther out, other birds swim and dive. Most of these water birds belong to four bird **orders:** ducks and their relatives; cranes and rails; storks and herons; and pelicans.

Ducks, geese, and swans

Ducks, geese, and swans (order Anseriformes) are medium-sized or large birds with webbed feet. They are good swimmers and find food by diving or dabbling—stretching their necks down into the water. Most of them mainly eat plants.

Ducks, geese, and swans lay their eggs in nests on the ground. Many of them are strong fliers, and geese especially fly on long **migrations.** They often fly in a "V" shape, each goose flying in the slipstream, or current of moving air, created by the one in front. This means the birds do not have to use as much energy.

Cranes and rails

Cranes and rails (order Gruiformes) include some common birds such as coots. But many birds in this group are **endangered.** They are ground-feeding or water-feeding birds. Unlike most water birds, they have unwebbed or slightly webbed feet or fleshy **lobes** on their feet. None of these birds has a **crop.**

Swans are strong fliers but have trouble taking off. They have to run over the water to gather speed for takeoff.

16

Storks, herons, and flamingos

Storks, herons and flamingos (order Ciconiiformes) are all long-legged birds that feed in shallow water. The group also includes spoonbills and ibises. Herons like to eat fish, which they spear using their daggerlike beak. They have a kind of trigger in their neck, which allows them to suddenly shoot their head forward to stab their **prey.** Flamingos feed with their heads upside down, filtering tiny creatures from the water. Storks and their relatives use sticks to make large, untidy nests in high places. In some countries, they nest on the roofs of buildings.

*Flamingoes feed in huge **flocks** on salty lakes. As many as a million flamingoes may gather in one place to feed.*

Pelicans and their relatives

Pelicans, gannets, cormorants, and frigate birds (order Pelecaniformes) are seabirds as well as water birds. Pelicans have webbing between all four toes and a pouch in their throats. They use the pouch as a fishing net. Cormorants use a small throat sac to help them cool off in hot weather. Male frigate birds have a big red pouch that they blow up like a balloon to impress females.

Birds in this group are mostly fish-eaters. Frigate birds use pirate tactics. They dive-bomb birds that have caught food and try to make them drop their catch.

Seabirds and Shore Birds

Most seabirds belong to one of three bird **orders:** gulls and waders, tube-nosed birds, and penguins.

Gulls and waders

This order of birds (Charadriiformes) includes seabirds such as gulls and terns, shorebirds such as sandpipers and plovers, and swimming birds such as puffins and auks. They do not look similar, but they are grouped together because they have similar skulls, backbones, and voice boxes.

Terns and auks eat fish, but gulls are often **scavengers,** feeding on almost anything left by others. Waders feed on shores and in shallow water, digging in soft mud for worms and other creatures. Gulls and waders nest on the ground, often in small hollows scraped by the birds.

Skimmers are close relatives of gulls. They feed by skimming low, with the bottom part of their beaks in the water. If they feel a fish, they snap it up.

Tube-nosed birds

Tube-nosed birds include albatrosses (order Ciconiiformes) and petrels and shearwaters (order Procellariiformes). Most animals cannot drink seawater because of the salt in it. Seabirds have glands in their noses that can remove the salt, and these glands are particularly big in tube-nosed birds. Many tube-nosed birds spend almost their whole lives feeding on the open ocean, coming to land only to **breed.**

Penguins

More than any other birds, penguins have made the sea their home. They cannot fly, and their wings have become short flippers that they use for swimming. Penguins live mostly in cold seas in the southern hemisphere. As protection against the cold, they have short, furlike feathers and a thick layer of fat, or blubber.

Penguins come to shore mainly to breed. They usually breed in **colonies,** laying one or two eggs on a heap of stones or in a burrow. Emperor and king penguins make no nest at all. Male emperor penguins put the single egg on their feet and cover it with a special flap of skin to keep it warm.

Marathon migration

Many birds **migrate** each year. They breed in cooler climates and then migrate in autumn to warmer places, where there is more food during the winter. Many birds migrate long distances, but Arctic terns fly farthest of all. They spend half the year in the Arctic, then fly across the world to the Antarctic, That's a one-way trip of almost 10,000 miles (16,000 kilometers)!

The female emperor penguin lays a single egg and then returns to the sea to look for food, leaving the egg with the male. He balances the egg on his feet, keeping it off the cold ground. When it hatches two months later, the female returns to help feed the chick.

Birds of Prey

Birds of **prey** are birds that catch animals or other birds for food. They have strong talons, or claws, for gripping their prey and hooked beaks that are good for tearing flesh. There are two **orders:** the hawks and falcons, which mostly hunt by day, and the owls, which usually hunt by night.

Hawks and falcons

Eagles, buzzards, hawks, falcons, and Old World vultures all belong to the Falconiformes order of birds. Old World vultures do not usually catch their own prey. They eat carrion, or dead animals. All hawks and falcons have excellent eyesight, and some vultures also have a good sense of smell.

Most hawks and falcons swoop down on their prey, grab it in their strong talons, and kill it with their sharp beaks. Some birds hunt from a perch. Others glide and soar over an area, looking for prey. Falcons dive on to other flying birds from a height. They reach speeds of up to 80 miles (130 kilometers) an hour. The prey is hit so hard that the impact kills it.

Ospreys hunt fish. They plunge into the water, talons first, when they see a likely meal. Fish are slippery creatures, so ospreys have studs on their toes for extra grip.

Owls can lay up to twelve eggs. The eggs do not all hatch at once. If there is not enough food to feed all the young, the smallest ones do not get as much food. Eventually they die and are eaten by the others.

Owls

Like hawks and falcons, owls (order Strigiformes) have hooked beaks and strong talons. But they look very different.

An owl has two large eyes in a round or heart-shaped face. Its eyes are designed to see well in very dim light. But even more important for night hunting are its ears, which are hidden under the feathers just below the eyes. The shape of the owl's face is designed to collect sounds and focus them on the ears. The ears can also tell where a sound is coming from. In territory it knows well, an owl can hunt in the dark using its hearing alone.

An owl's wing-feathers have soft fringes at the tips, which soften the sound the owl makes as it flaps its wings. This means that the owl's victims do not hear it coming. It also allows the owl to hear the movements of its prey.

Owls usually eat their prey whole, but they cannot **digest** the animal's bones or fur. So after they have digested a meal, owls cough up a small pellet of this undigested matter. Scientists often study these pellets to find out what an owl has been eating.

While many birds are brilliant fliers, none are more impressive than swifts and hummingbirds (**order** Apodiformes). Swifts spend almost their whole lives in flight, catching insects in their mouths as they flit through the air. Hummingbirds are far better than other birds at hovering in one place, and they can fly backward. Nightjars are aerial acrobats similar to swifts, but as their name suggests, they hunt at night.

Swifts and hummingbirds

Swifts and hummingbirds are related by their short legs and tiny feet. Some swifts have such small legs and feet that they cannot walk on flat ground.

Swifts are small birds with long, pointed wings. They catch insects, sleep, and even **mate** in the air. The only time they land is when they are nesting. Swifts' nests are usually high up, sometimes on the roof of a building. The nests are made from small twigs and other material, held together with **saliva.**

The nests of cave swiftlets in Southeast Asia are made completely of saliva. In China, people make cave swiftlet nests into bird's nest soup.

Hummingbirds are colorful birds with long bills. Their main food is **nectar,** which they suck from flowers with their tubelike tongues. They also eat insects. They build tiny cup-shaped nests, which they stick together using spiders' webs.

Some hummingbirds live in tropical areas, where there are flowers all year, but others **migrate.** A hummingbird's wings beat very fast—up to 80 times a second. When they hover, hummingbirds rotate their wings as they beat, moving them in a figure-eight pattern. This is why they can hover so well.

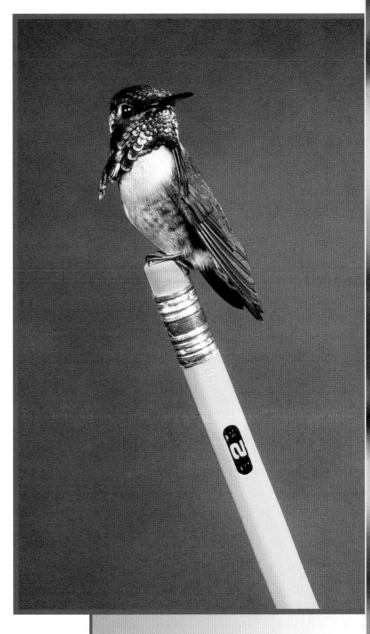

All hummingbirds are small, but some are really tiny. The bee hummingbird is less than 2.5 inches (6 centimeters) from beak to tail, and its body is not much bigger than that of a bee.

Nightjars

Like swifts, most nightjars catch insects while in flight. They hunt mostly at night, and moths are the main food for many **species.** Nightjars have small beaks, but they can open their mouths very wide. That is why some species are known as frogmouths. During the day, nightjars rest on the ground or in trees, relying on their excellent **camouflage** to keep them safe from enemies.

Woodpeckers and kingfishers belong to two **orders** of birds that lay their eggs in holes. Many kingfishers dig their holes in earthen banks or rotten trees. Woodpeckers use their strong bills to hack out nesting holes in tree trunks.

A common kingfisher plunge-dives for food. Although kingfishers are common in many parts of the world, the white-collared kingfisher of Arabia is one of the rarest birds on Earth. Only about 50 pairs are known to survive.

Kingfishers and relatives

Kingfishers (order Coraciiformes) are often brightly colored. This group also includes bee-eaters, rollers, and hornbills. Most perch and watch for food and then swoop or dive to catch it.

Rollers swoop down on insects or small creatures and sometimes also eat fruit. Kingfishers are mostly water birds, diving from a perch to stab fish with their beaks. Bee-eaters catch flying insects, especially bees and wasps.

Kingfishers and their relatives lay between two and seven eggs. Their young are born blind and helpless. Female hornbills use mud to block the entrance to their nest holes, leaving only a narrow opening. The mother then lays her eggs and keeps them warm. The male feeds her through the small nest opening. After the eggs hatch, the mother stays sealed in with the nestlings until they are no longer helpless. Then at last she breaks the nest open.

Woodpeckers

Woodpeckers and their relatives (order Piciformes) include jacamars, puffbirds, barbets, honeyguides, and toucans. They are often brightly colored or have strong markings. All of them have feet with two backward-pointing toes and two toes pointing forward. They nest in holes and lay pure-white eggs.

Woodpeckers feed at tree trunks, poking their beaks into cracks in the bark and licking out insects with their super-long tongues. Woodpeckers' stiff tails help them to balance on tree trunks as they move around. Jacamars and puffbirds chase after flying insects, like bee-eaters do, while barbets eat fruit and insects.

Honeyguides like to eat the wax from bees' nests. But they can't open the nests themselves, so they get help. If a honeyguide finds a bees' nest, it flies around until it sees a large animal such as a honey badger. It then guides the animal to the bees' nest, stopping and calling on the way. Once the badger finds the nest and hungrily breaks it open, the honeyguide can feed on the wax.

Not all woodpeckers eat only insects. Sapsuckers also drill holes in tree trunks and suck up the sweet sap.

Parrots, Pigeons, and Cuckoos

Parrots, pigeons, and cuckoos are all woodland birds, but they belong to different **orders.**

Parrots have often been kept as pets, because they are good at imitating human speech. Unlike most birds, they can hold food in one foot to eat it.

Parrots and their relatives

The parrot order, Psittaciformes, includes cockatoos, parakeets, lovebirds, and macaws. They are noisy, colorful tropical birds that live mainly in forests. Parrots have a curved beak strong enough to crack a brazil nut and strong feet that they use to help them feed and climb.

Parrots eat plant foods: seeds, fruits, nuts, and **nectar.** They often feed in large **flocks.** Parakeets feed in flocks of up to a million! Many **species** nest in holes, either in trees or in the ground.

More than 30 parrot species are **endangered,** many of them because their forest homes have been cut down. The kakapo is a rare New Zealand parrot that was almost wiped out by cats, which were brought to New Zealand by the first European settlers.

Pigeons and doves

Pigeons (order Columbiformes) are a familiar sight in most towns and cities. They are feral, which means they were once bred by people but then escaped into the wild. Doves and wild pigeons look similar to feral pigeons. They are mainly seed-eaters.

Pigeons build nests of twigs and lay one or two eggs. The babies are born helpless, and at first they are fed on pigeon milk. This is a creamy substance, which the parents make in their **crops**.

Cuckoos

Cuckoos and their relatives (order Cuculiformes) are a varied group, but they all have similar feet. They include the noisy, colorful turacos and a few larger ground birds such as the roadrunner. Cuckoos are insect-eaters. Some species specialize in eating nasty-tasting caterpillars that other animals won't eat.

Passenger pigeons were the most common birds ever known. Over five billion of them lived in North America. But they were good to eat, so people killed them in huge numbers. The last passenger pigeon died in a zoo in 1914.

About half of all cuckoo species lay their eggs in other birds' nests. The cuckoo egg hatches quickly and the babies push the other baby birds out of the nest. The baby cuckoo then gets all the food that the adult birds bring to the nest.

Water-carriers

Sandgrouse are desert birds related to pigeons. They have to fly long distances each day to drink. When they are first born, sandgrouse babies cannot get water for themselves. So the father bird flies to a water hole and dips his belly feathers in the water. These feathers are specially designed to soak up water. He then flies back to the nest, and the young suck water from the feathers.

Is It a Bird?

Today there are no other animals that could be confused with birds. Like birds, insects and bats can fly. But insects have no feathers or beak, and most are too small to be mistaken for birds. Bats have furry bodies and leathery wings rather than ones made from feathers.

Millions of years ago in the Cretaceous period—between 145 and 65 million years ago—things were not so straightforward. There were some early types of birds, such as *Archaeopteryx*, which had feathers and wings. But there were also other animals that could fly and other animals that had feathers. The other flyers were winged reptiles called **pterosaurs,** which had wings made from leathery skin. The feathered animals were certain **species** of dinosaur, which could not fly but were covered in feathers.

Pterosaurs

Pterosaur means "winged lizard." Pterosaurs were the first large flying animals. They first appeared when dinosaurs still roamed the earth. Their leathery wings were supported mostly by an enormously long fourth finger bone. The other three fingers formed a claw on the joint of the wing.

Rhamphorhynchus *was a pterosaur. It had a long, bony tail to help it steer. The elongated fourth finger held the leathery wing stiff.*

There were many different pterosaurs. Some had teeth and jaws as other reptiles did, but some had a toothless, beaklike jaw. The biggest pterosaurs were really huge. *Quetzalcoatlus* measured 39 feet (12 meters) from wing tip to wing tip—as big as a small plane! The largest pterosaurs probably spent most of their time soaring and gliding, but the small pterosaurs could flap their wings and fly quite well.

Feathered dinosaurs

In recent years, many **fossils** of feathered dinosaurs have been found in China. These dinosaurs could not fly. They looked similar to small relatives of *Tyrannosaurus rex* but with a feathery covering.

The fossils are about 125 million years old, which is several million years younger than the fossils of *Archaeopteryx*. So these dinosaurs were living at the same time as the **ancestors** of today's flying birds.

This is an artist's idea of how Archaeopteryx *might have looked. Unlike modern birds,* Archaeopteryx *had claws at the front of its wings. These might have helped it to climb trees.*

Glossary

adaptation special feature that helps an organism to survive in its habitat

ancestor relative from long in the past

breed to produce babies

camouflage color, shape, or pattern that disguises an animal against its background

class level of classification grouping between phylum and order. Birds make up a class.

colony large group of animals or plants, often of the same species, living together in a small area

crop pouch inside a bird's mouth usually used to feed babies

digest to break down food for use by the body

digestive system part of an animal's body that breaks down food so that it can be used by the body

endangered in danger of becoming extinct, or dying out as a species

family level of classification grouping between order and genus

flock large gathering of birds, usually of one species

fossil remains of ancient living creatures (usually formed from bones or shells) found in rocks

genus (plural is **genera**) level of classification grouping between family and species

kingdom highest level of classification. All animals make up one kingdom.

lobe rounded projection or division of a body part

mate to come together to make babies; or, an animal's partner

migrate to move from one place to another for part of the year

migration movement of birds from one place to another for part of the year

nectar sweet liquid produced by flowers

order level of classification grouping between class and family

passerine individual of the largest order of birds, which includes crows, finches, sparrows, and wrens

phylum (plural is **phyla**) level of classification grouping between kingdom and class

plumage feathers

predator animal that hunts and eats other animals

prey animal that is hunted for food by another animal

pterosaur extinct type of winged dinosaurs that had leathery wings instead of feathers

saliva spit

scavenger animal which does not hunt its own food but looks for leftovers from other animals

species lowest level of classification grouping. Only members of the same species can reproduce together.

vertebrate animal with an internal backbone. All birds are vertebrates.

More Books to Read

National Wildlife Federation Staff. *Birds, Birds, Birds.* Broomall, Penn.: Chelsea House Publishers, 1999.

Parker, Steve. *Adaptation.* Chicago: Heinemann Library, 2000.

Wallace, Holly. *Classification.* Chicago: Heinemann Library, 2000.

Index